W9-BVC-096

3-99

Venus Flytraps

by Kathleen V. Kudlinski
photographs by Jerome Wexler

Lerner Publications Company • Minneapolis, Minnesota

For Ryan Beal, who does not eat flies
—KVK

Thanks to our series consultant, Sharyn Fenwick, elementary science/math specialist. Mrs. Fenwick was the winner of the National Science Teachers Association 1991 Distinguished Teaching Award. She also was the recipient of the Presidential Award for Excellence in Math and Science Teaching, representing the state of Minnesota at the elementary level in 1992.

Additional photographs are reproduced with the permission of the following sources: © Robert and Linda Mitchell, pp. 6, 7, 9, 25, 27; © John Netherton, pp. 10, 22; © David Sieren/Visuals Unlimited, pp. 20, 41, 42; Jim Simondet/ Independent Picture Service, p. 26. Illustrations by Laura Westlund, p. 5; Bryan Liedahl, pp. 15, 34, and 36. Thanks to Ryan Johnson and Jim Kiner, who modeled for this book.

Early Bird Nature Books were conceptualized by Ruth Berman and designed by Steve Foley. Series editor is Joelle Goldman.

Website address: www.lernerbooks.com

Library of Congress Cataloging-in-Publication Data

Kudlinski, Kathleen V.
   Venus flytraps / by Kathleen V. Kudlinski ; photographs by Jerome Wexler.
      p. cm. — (Early bird nature books)
   Includes index.
   Summary: Describes the physical characteristics of these carnivorous plants, where they live, and how they trap and digest their insect prey.
   ISBN 0-8225-3015-5 (alk. paper)
   1. Venus's flytrap—Juvenile literature. 2. Venus's flytrap—Life cycles—Juvenile literature. [1. Venus's flytrap.] I. Wexler, Jerome, ill. II. Title. III. Series.
QK495.D76K84 1998
583'.75—dc21   97–42912

Manufactured in the United States of America
1 2 3 4 5 6 – JR – 03 02 01 00 99 98

Contents

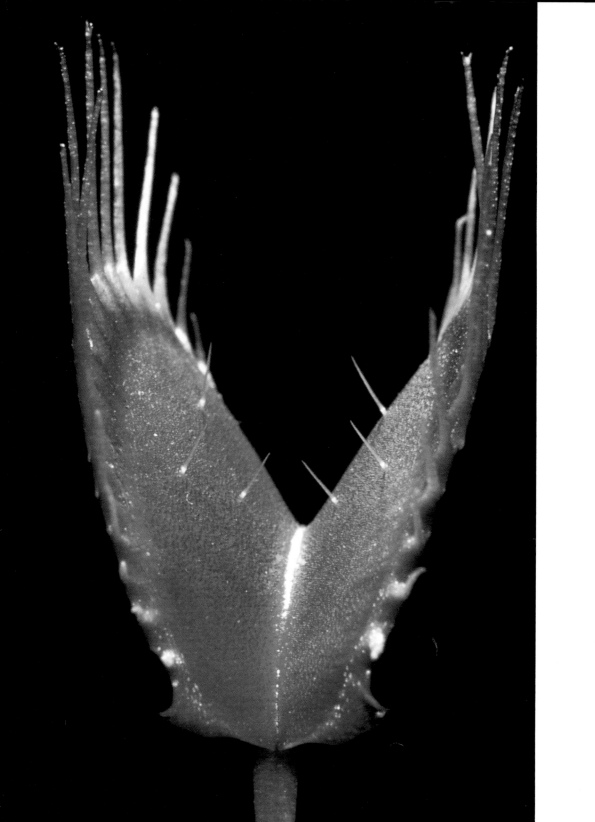

Alaska
(U.S.)

CANADA

N

Venus flytraps grow wild in North and South Carolina, in the southeastern United States. The green area shows where Venus flytraps live.

UNITED STATES

MEXICO

Be a Word Detective

Can you find these words as you read about the Venus flytrap's life? Be a detective and try to figure out what they mean. You can turn to the glossary on page 46 for help.

bog	**nectar**	**pistil**
carnivorous	**nitrogen**	**pollen**
carbon dioxide	**ovules**	**rhizomes**
chlorophyll	**petals**	**stamens**

Chapter 1

Most plants are not dangerous. Do you think this plant's leaf would hurt a fly?

A Hungry Plant

The day is hot. A fly buzzes over the wet, soggy ground. The fly is looking for breakfast. It sees a bright red leaf. The leaf has two parts. The fly smells something sweet and buzzes closer. It lands to lick at the sweet, gooey liquid on the leaf's edges.

Snap! The leaf slams shut on the fly. Sharp points on the edges of the leaf fit together to make a cage. The fly wiggles and pushes, but the plant will not let the fly out. The leaf closes tighter. In a few minutes, the fly stops moving. Everything is quiet.

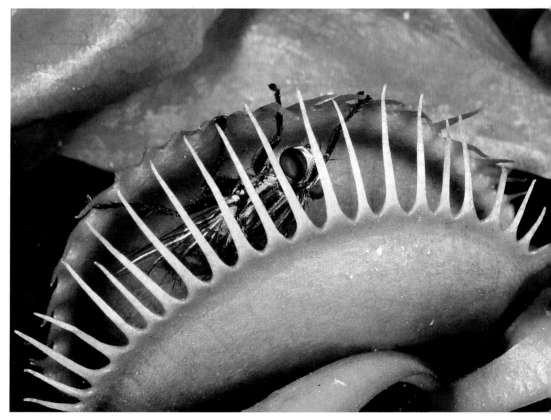

The leaf closes so quickly, the fly can't get away. The trap snaps shut in less than one second.

Ten days later, the leaf cage opens. The fly is dead. All that is left of the fly is a dry shell. Wind blows the fly parts away. The leaf waits. It is ready for another meal.

This fly is dead. The plant has eaten the soft parts of the fly's body.

The Venus flytrap is famous for catching flies. But flytraps eat mostly crawling insects, like ants.

This plant is a Venus flytrap. Its name tells us that it traps flies. A Venus flytrap will also eat an ant or a bee. It will eat any little visitor that steps on its special leaves. The Venus flytrap is carnivorous (car-NIH-vuh-russ). That means it eats animals.

Not many plants eat animals. Venus flytraps are unusual plants. They are also rare. These plants grow wild only in North and South Carolina. They live in bogs. Bogs are places where the ground is so wet it is like a sponge dripping with water.

This South Carolina bog is home to many unusual carnivorous plants, including the Venus flytrap.

The Venus flytrap's scientific name is Dionaea muscipula.
It grows to be 5 or 6 inches high.

A Venus flytrap sits flat on the ground.
From its center grow 3 to 20 stems. At the end
of each stem is a leaf with two parts. The
leaves are green on the outside and red on the
inside. Spines grow from the leaves' edges. The
spines spread out like the rays of the sun. A tall
flower stem grows from the middle of the plant.
The flowers at the end of this stem are small
and white.

A flytrap will "bite" your finger without hurting you.
But the flytrap's bite will kill something smaller.

The Venus flytrap is pretty, but it is dangerous. It would not hurt anyone as big as you. But it will kill and eat anything small enough to fall into its trap.

First the Venus flytrap has to grow big enough to catch a fly.

Chapter 2

If this flytrap seed falls onto the moss of a bog, the seed will grow. What is the first part of a plant to grow from a seed?

A Flytrap Grows

 A small black seed falls onto the wet moss in a bog. The seed's shiny coat gets wet and starts to soften. The coat splits. One tiny root pushes out of the seed. In a day or so, the root pushes down through the moss into the wet soil below. In another day, more roots grow. The roots have tiny hairs on them. These root hairs suck water and chemicals from the soil.

Two small leaves grow up from the seed. They reach toward the sunlight. In another week, more leaves sprout. These leaves are bigger. They are red on top and green below. These leaves will grow into the traps that eat animals.

This tiny, sprouting plant doesn't look deadly. When it grows bigger, it will grow leaves that can kill any insect that falls into its traps.

Rhizomes are stems that grow underground. Some new Venus flytraps grow from rhizomes, not from seeds.

This is one way that a Venus flytrap plant grows. But a Venus flytrap doesn't have to grow from a seed. There is another way that new flytrap plants can grow.

In the soggy soil of the bog, special stems grow from an old flytrap plant. These stems are called rhizomes (RY-zomes). They do not grow up through the soil like most plant stems. Instead, rhizomes grow sideways underground.

This Venus flytrap has been dug up from the soil. You can see the rhizomes growing out from the plant.

At the tip of a rhizome, new leaves sprout. Roots grow down. Soon, a whole new plant is growing there. This plant did not grow from a seed. This new flytrap grew from an old flytrap plant.

Spread your fingers wide. Your hand is about the size of a full-grown Venus flytrap. In just a few months, the plant grew to that size from a tiny sprout.

Chapter 3

Sunlight helps green plants grow. What does a green plant make from the sunshine?

A Flytrap's Own Food

 All plants need food to grow. Green plants like the flytrap can make their own food. They use water and chemicals from the soil. They use sunshine and the air around them.

On the bottom of the flytrap's leaves are tiny holes. Air flows in and out through these holes. One important part of this air is the gas called carbon dioxide (dy-AHK-side). The flytrap plant uses carbon dioxide to make food.

A new flytrap leaf is green because the leaf contains chlorophyll.

Chlorophyll (KLOR-uh-fihl) is the bright green chemical that gives plants their color. But chlorophyll isn't just for color. Chlorophyll is a working chemical. It makes food.

Chlorophyll mixes with water and chemicals from the soil. It uses carbon dioxide from the air. And it takes energy from the sun shining on the plant's leaves and stems. Chlorophyll uses the energy to change the chemicals into food.

All plants with chlorophyll can make food this way. Trees and mosses make their own food. Green seaweeds and cactus make their own food, too. Flytraps are green plants. Their leaves contain chlorophyll. But they are not like these other plants. Flytraps can't make enough food from just carbon dioxide, water, sunshine, and chemicals from the soil. Venus flytraps need meat to stay healthy.

Dandelions are like Venus flytraps, because they have chlorophyll in their green leaves and stems. But dandelions do not eat meat.

Venus flytraps grow in soggy, mossy soil called peat.

Do you know why Venus flytraps trap flies? Remember that to make food, chlorophyll needs the chemicals that come into a plant's roots. Those chemicals come from the soil. The soil that Venus flytraps live in is soggy bog soil. Bog soil is missing one important chemical. This chemical is called nitrogen (NY-truh-juhn).

20

The plant food we use in our gardens has nitrogen in it. Most soil has some nitrogen. But watery bog soil has almost no nitrogen. Without enough nitrogen, flytrap plants can't make all the food they need to live.

Like Venus flytraps, pitcher plants live in bogs. Pitcher plants are also carnivorous.

A trap cannot close around a catch that is too big. If this frog is strong enough, it may be able to escape.

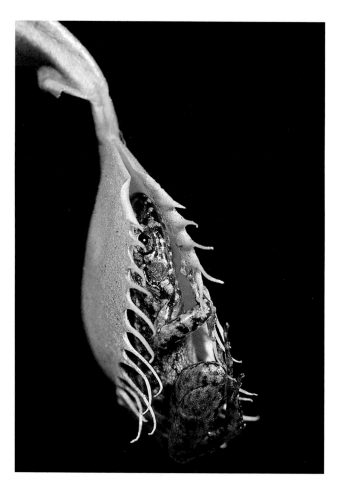

That's why Venus flytraps are hungry. They are hungry for nitrogen. Animals have nitrogen in their bodies. Elephants and swans and flies all have nitrogen. But flytraps need just an extra bit of nitrogen to make their food. So they trap just tiny animals, like flies.

Chapter 4

A trap catches flying insects, but it doesn't have to chase them. Why would a fly walk into this trap?

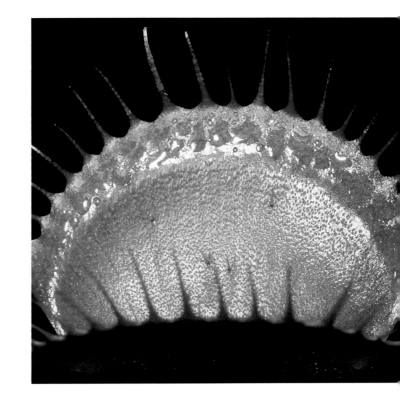

The Trap Snaps!

 A Venus flytrap does not have to chase its meals. Flies and ants and wasps and other insects come right to it. The plant makes a sweet-smelling liquid on its leaves. The insects come for a drink. Instead, they get a surprise.

Each trap has six or more stiff hairs. Half are on one half of the leaf. Half are on the other. They work like triggers. When an insect comes for a drink, it steps on one of these trigger hairs.

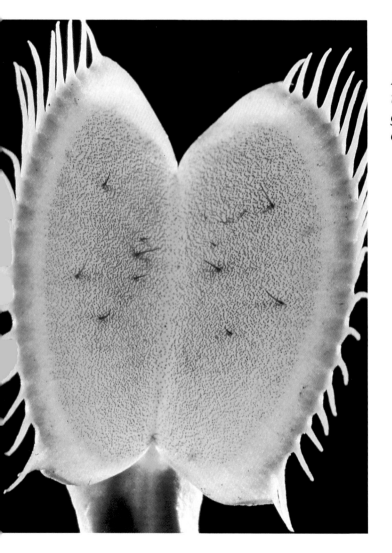

If one trigger hair is touched, the trap gets ready to close on its meal.

If a second trigger hair is touched within a few seconds of the first, the trap quickly closes.

The trap does not shut yet. But if a second hair is stepped on, the plant knows the insect is big enough for a good meal. The trap snaps shut as fast as you can blink your eye.

Your hands make a good trap. So do the leaves of a Venus flytrap.

To see how the trap works, hold your hands out. Put your wrists together. Your wrists are like the plant's stem. Your hands are like the two halves of the leaf. Imagine an ant crawling across one of your palms. Quickly fold your hands together. The ant would be stuck inside your hands. It might try to crawl out the edges. Next fit your fingers together and tighten them. The ant couldn't get out now, could it?

When a leaf shuts, the long stiff spines on its edges fit together like your fingers. They make a cage. The fly can still see out through the spines. A teeny, tiny fly can still get away. A big one gets stuck. It wiggles, and it touches more of the trigger hairs. That makes the trap shut tighter.

A flytrap doesn't want to bother with a meal that is too small. It gives a small insect a chance to escape.

This flytrap wasn't fooled by a seed of wheat. The trap opened to let the seed fall out.

If a piece of dirt falls into the trap, the trap closes. But dirt doesn't wiggle. The trap doesn't shut tighter. Instead, in a few minutes, the trap opens and the dirt falls out. A Venus flytrap eats only living things like flies.

Slowly the edges of the leaf press together around the fly. The leaf closes until no more light can go into the cage. No air can go in either. The fly cannot breathe. It dies.

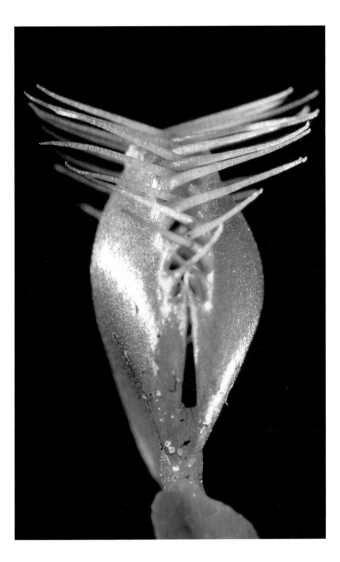

The more the insect wiggles, the tighter the trap closes. This time, the fly can't get out.

When the fly stops moving, a special juice oozes from inside the flytrap's leaves. The juice fills the space around the dead fly's body. This juice turns the soft parts of the fly's body into liquid. There was nitrogen in the fly's body. Now the nitrogen is in the juice. In the next 8 to 10 days, the juice and its nitrogen soak back into the leaf. Then the plant has everything it needs to make its own food.

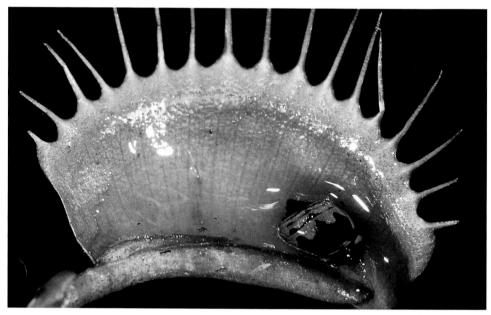

A leaf has been cut in half to show the juice and the dead yellow jacket inside.

Each leaf can eat just three times. But a plant keeps growing new leaves.

After the plant has eaten, the trap opens wide again. The leaf is ready to catch its next meal.

A trap can shut and make its special juice only three times. After that, the leaf turns black and dies. The nitrogen it added to the plant helped the plant make more food. The plant uses this food to keep growing. It grows more roots. It grows longer rhizomes. It grows more stalks and leaves, and flowers, too.

Chapter 5

Flowers bloom high above the Venus flytrap's traps. Why do insects like to visit a flytrap's flowers?

Flytrap Flowers

 A Venus flytrap doesn't kill every visitor that flies to it. The plant needs living visitors, too. These other visitors help the plant make seeds.

In the spring and summer, one or more stalks grow from the middle of the Venus flytrap plant. They grow and grow until they are about a foot taller than the traps. At the very top of each stalk, 2 to 15 flowers bloom.

Every flower has five white petals around its yellow center. Inside this center, a tasty liquid called nectar is hidden. Flying insects come to drink the nectar.

The Venus flytrap's tiny flowers bloom in May and June. These flowers up close look larger than their normal size.

When a bee or wasp or other thirsty insect steps on a flower, the insect doesn't get trapped. It gets a nice drink. And it gets covered with tiny yellow grains called pollen.

The bee knows the flower's nectar tastes sweet. As the bee drinks, pollen sticks to the bee's legs and body.

In these photos taken up close, you can see the yellow grains of pollen on the flower's stamens and the bee's leg.

This pollen dust is made by the parts of the flower called the stamens (STAY-mehnz). The stamens are short stems near the center of the flower. The pollen from the stamens sticks all over the insect's body.

One drink isn't enough. As the bee flies from flower to flower, it moves pollen from one flower to another.

The nectar is so tasty that the insect wants to drink more. The insect moves to another flytrap flower for another drink. It squirms deep into the flower to get every last drop. As the insect squirms, some of the pollen on its body rubs off.

36

At the very center of the flower is a stem called the pistil. The pistil is sticky. Pollen grains stick to it after the insect flies away. The insect doesn't move the pollen on purpose. It is an accident, but it is a very important accident.

The flower's sticky pistil collects the pollen an insect leaves behind.

After the pollen reaches a flower's pistil, seeds grow inside the pistil and form a bulge.

When a pollen grain lands on a pistil, the grain starts to grow. Before a day passes, a tube grows from the grain down into the pistil. Down inside the pistil are ovules (AHV-yoolz). Ovules are baby seeds. When a pollen grain's tube reaches an ovule, the ovule has been pollinated. Pollinated ovules can grow into seeds.

The flower has done its work. The petals fall off. The nectar dries up. Inside a tightly closed seed case, shiny black seeds grow. One seed grows for every ovule that was pollinated.

The seed case turns black and starts to open. Now you can see the seeds inside it.

In a month or two, the seed case opens. Rain can splash the seeds out. A running animal can knock them out. Strong winds can whip the seed case around. The seeds scatter, or they simply drop to the soggy ground below.

In a few weeks, tiny roots push out from each seed. The roots reach down into the wet soil, and a new Venus flytrap grows.

Each one of these seeds can grow into a new Venus flytrap plant.

Chapter 6

Venus flytraps grow in this Carolina bog. Do you think many Venus flytraps grow wild?

Flytraps at Home

 Not many Venus flytraps are growing wild. That is because there are not many places for them to grow. The plants like only the boggy soils in North and South Carolina. Many bogs in these states have been drained to make farmland.

Laws have been made to protect this plant. Even so, a Venus flytrap growing in nature is a rare sight.

Other bogs are in parks. The bogs and all the bog plants are protected there. But sometimes people come into the parks and dig up the Venus flytrap plants. This is stealing. These people sell the plants to make money.

If you see a Venus flytrap in a store, ask where the plant came from. Some farms grow flytraps in soggy, boggy fields kept just for them. If your Venus flytrap came from a bog farm, take the plant home and feed it well. Keep the soil very wet, and it will live a long time.

A Venus flytrap indoors will need lots of sunlight, rainwater, and live food, such as spiders and ants.

On Sharing a Book

As you know, adults greatly influence a child's attitude toward reading. When a child sees you read, or when you share a book with a child, you're sending a message that reading is important. Show the child that reading a book together is important to you. Find a comfortable, quiet place. Turn off the television and limit other distractions, such as telephone calls.

Be prepared to start slowly. Take turns reading parts of this book. Stop and talk about what you're reading. Talk about the photographs. You may find that much of the shared time is spent discussing just a few pages. This discussion time is valuable for both of you, so don't move through the book too quickly. If the child begins to lose interest, stop reading. Continue sharing the book at another time. When you do pick up the book again, be sure to revisit the parts you have already read. Most importantly, enjoy the book!

Be a Vocabulary Detective

You will find a word list on page 5. Words selected for this list are important to the understanding of the topic of this book. Encourage the child to be a word detective and search for the words as you read the book together. Talk about what the words mean and how they are used in the sentence. Do any of these words have more than one meaning? You will find these words defined in a glossary on page 46.

What about Questions?

Use questions to make sure the child understands the information in this book. Here are some suggestions:

> What did this paragraph tell us? What does this picture show? What do you think we'll learn about next? Where do Venus flytraps grow? How are Venus flytraps different from the plants you see every day? How are they the same? What does a flytrap seedling need to grow? What are the parts of the Venus flytrap's flowers? Why does the flytrap plant eat insects? How does the Venus flytrap catch an insect? What is your favorite part of the book? Why?

If the child has questions, don't hesitate to respond with questions of your own such as: What do *you* think? Why? What is it that you don't know? If the child can't remember certain facts, turn to the index.

Introducing the Index

The index is an important learning tool. It helps readers get information quickly without searching throughout the whole book. Turn to the index on page 48. Choose an entry, such as *stems,* and ask the child to use the index to find the name of the flytrap's special stems that grow sideways underground. Repeat this exercise with as many entries as you like. Ask the child to point out the differences between an index and a glossary. (The index helps readers find information quickly, while the glossary tells readers what words mean.)

All the World in Metric!

Although our monetary system is in metric units (based on multiples of 10), the United States is one of the few countries in the world that does not use the metric system of measurement. Here are some conversion activities you and the child can do using a calculator:

WHEN YOU KNOW:	MULTIPLY BY:	TO FIND:
inches	2.54	centimeters
gallons	3.787	liters
pounds	0.454	kilograms

Activities

Go to the library and read about other carnivorous plants. What do the pitcher plant, sundew, cobra lily, and bladderwort have in common with the Venus flytrap? How are the plants different?

Invent an imaginary carnivorous plant. Give the plant a name. How does it attract and trap insects? Draw a picture of the plant in its habitat. Label the plant's parts.

Try an experiment to see how plants grow in different types of soil. Fill one flower pot with potting soil and another with peat moss. Plant the same kind of flower or grass seeds in both pots. Keep the soil moist. As you watch the seedlings sprout, note the size, color, and strength of the plants' stems and leaves. Do the plants grow better in one pot than in the other? When the seedlings are two weeks old, begin feeding them with small amounts of nitrogen-rich fertilizer. After two more weeks, again observe the plants' stems and leaves. Did the fertilizer help the plants grow? Why?

Glossary

bog—an area of land that has very wet, spongy soil

carnivorous (car-NIH-vuh-russ)—meat-eating

carbon dioxide (dy-AHK-side)—a part of air that plants use to make food

chlorophyll (KLOR-uh-fihl)—the green substance found in a plant that makes food for the plant

nectar—a sweet liquid that flowers make

nitrogen (NY-truh-juhn)—a gas that is part of the air and is found in all living things

ovules (AHV-yoolz)—baby seeds

petals—the colored outer parts of a flower

pistil—the part of a flower where seeds grow

pollen—yellow powder from a flower that is needed to make seeds

rhizomes (RY-zomes)—stems that grow sideways underground

stamens (STAY-mehnz)—the parts of the flower where pollen grows

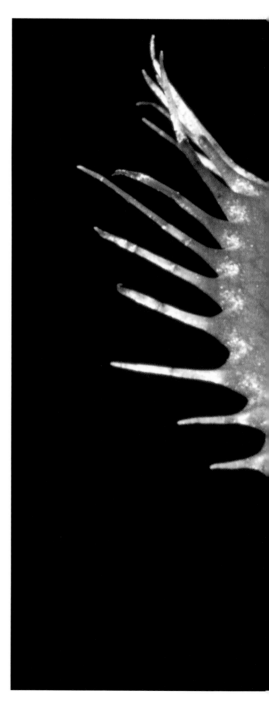

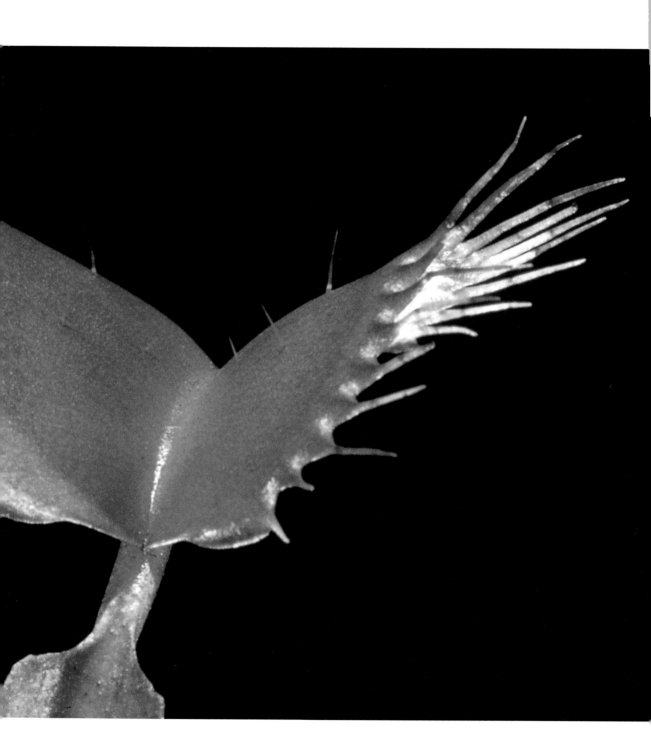

Index

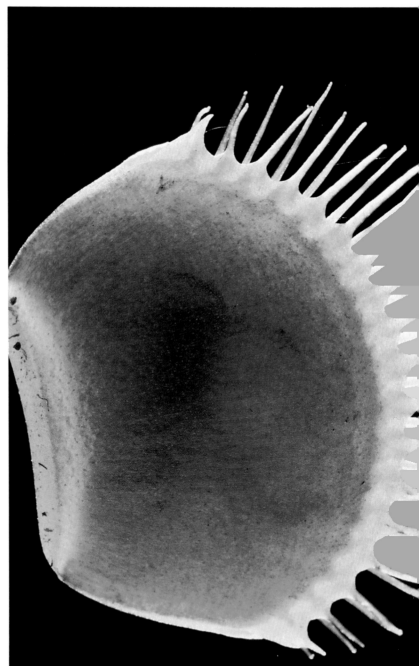